SRA®

MULTIPLE SKILLS
SERIES: Reading

Third Edition

Richard A. Boning

SRA McGraw-Hill

Columbus, Ohio

A Division of The **McGraw·Hill** *Companies*

SRA/McGraw-Hill

*A Division of The **McGraw·Hill** Companies*

Printed in the United States of America.

Send all inquiries to:
SRA/McGraw-Hill
8787 Orion Place
Columbus, OH 43240-4027

ISBN 0-02-688410-0

6 7 8 9 SCG 02 01

To the Teacher

PURPOSE

The *Multiple Skills Series* is a nonconsumable reading program designed to develop a cluster of key reading skills and to integrate these skills with each other and with the other language arts. *Multiple Skills* is also diagnostic, making it possible for you to identify specific types of reading skills that might be causing difficulty for individual students.

FOR WHOM

The twelve levels of the *Multiple Skills Series* are geared to students who comprehend on the pre-first- through ninth-grade reading levels.

- The Picture Level is for children who have not acquired a basic sight vocabulary.
- The Preparatory 1 Level is for children who have developed a limited basic sight vocabulary.
- The Preparatory 2 Level is for children who have a basic sight vocabulary but are not yet reading on the first-grade level.
- Books A through I are appropriate for students who can read on grade levels one through nine respectively. Because of their high interest level, the books may also be used effectively with students functioning at these levels of competence in other grades.

The **Multiple Skills Series Placement Tests** will help you determine the appropriate level for each student.

PLACEMENT TESTS

The Elementary Placement Test (for grades Pre-1 through 3) and the Midway Placement Tests (for grades 4–9) will help you place each student properly. The tests consist of representative units selected from the series. The test books contain two forms, X and Y. One form may be used for placement and the second as a posttest to measure progress. The tests are easy to administer and score. Blackline Masters are provided for worksheets and student performance profiles.

THE BOOKS

This third edition of the *Multiple Skills Series* maintains the quality and focus that have distinguished this program for over 25 years. The series includes four books at each level, Picture Level through Level I. Each book in the Picture Level through Level B contains 25 units. Each book in Level C through Level I contains 50 units. The units within each book increase in difficulty. The books within a level also increase in difficulty—Level A, Book 2 is slightly more difficult than Level A, Book 1, and so on. This gradual increase in difficulty permits students to advance from one book to the next and from one level to the next without frustration.

Each book contains an **About This Book** page, which explains the skills to the students and shows them how to approach reading the selections and questions. In the lowest levels, you should read About This Book to the children.

The questions that follow each unit are designed to develop specific reading skills. In the lowest levels, you should read the questions to the children.

In Levels A and B, the question pattern in each unit is
1. Title (main idea)
2. Stated detail
3. Stated detail
4. Inference or conclusion
5. Picture clue

The **Language Activity Pages** (LAP) in each level consist of four parts: Exercising Your Skill, Expanding Your Skill, Exploring Language, and Expressing Yourself. These pages lead the students beyond the book through a broadening spiral of writing, speaking, and other individual and group language activities that apply, extend, and integrate the skills being developed. You may use all, some, or none of the activities in any LAP; however, some LAP activities depend on preceding ones. In the lowest levels, you should read the LAPs to the children.

In Level A, each set of Language Activity Pages focuses on a particular skill developed through the book:

First LAP	Details
Second LAP	Picture interpretations
Third LAP	Main ideas
Last LAP	Inferences and conclusions

SESSIONS

The *Multiple Skills Series* is an individualized reading program that may be used with small groups or an entire class. Short sessions are the most effective. Use a short session every day or every other day, completing a few units in each session. Time allocated to the Language Activity Pages depends on the abilities of the individual students.

SCORING

Students should record their answers on the reproducible worksheets. The worksheets make scoring easier and provide uniform records of the children's work. Using worksheets also avoids consuming the books.

Because it is important for the students to know how they are progressing, you should score the units as soon as they've been completed. Then you can discuss the questions and activities with the students and encourage them to justify their responses. Many of the LAPs are open-ended and do not lend themselves to an objective score; for this reason, there are no answer keys for these pages.

When you read a story, you read words and sentences that belong together. They all help to tell about one **main idea**. Read this story. Think about what it is mainly about.

> Ann had a green plant. It began to look brown. She gave her plant water. She put it in the sun. Soon the plant was green again.

Do all of the sentences in the story tell about Ann's plant? Would "Ann's Plant" be a good title for the story? Figuring out what a story is mainly about is an important reading skill.

Another important reading skill is remembering the facts, or **details**, in a story. In the story above, what was the girl's name? What was wrong with her plant? A good reader pays attention to the facts.

A good reader also figures out **things that the writer does not say**. What did Ann do for her plant? Why do you think she did these things? The story does not tell you that green plants need water and sunlight, but you can figure this out from what the story tells you. Good readers think about what the story tells them. They figure things out as they read.

Sometimes a story has a **picture** to go with it. The picture may tell you things that the words do not. The picture can help tell the story.

In this book, there are twenty-five stories. Read each story and look at the picture that goes with it. Then choose a good **title**, or name, for the story. Answer the questions about what the story and the picture tell you.

Mrs. Green could not find her ring. She had put it on the TV. Now it was gone. She said, "I'll put another ring on the TV and see who takes it."

Mrs. Green was surprised. The window was open and a bird came into the house. It took the ring and went back to its nest in a tree. Mrs. Green's son went up the tree to look in the nest. In the nest he found both of his mother's rings.

1. The best title is—

    (A) Going to the Farm

    (B) The Lost Rings

    (C) Children Have Fun

    (D) Mrs. Green Goes Away

2. The bird went into—

    (A) a bus   (B) a train

    (C) Mrs. Green's   (D) Mrs. Green's car
        house

3. The bird put Mrs. Green's rings—

    (A) into a shoe   (B) in the grass

    (C) under a truck   (D) into its nest

4. The bird took—

    (A) two hats   (B) two rings

    (C) a toy   (D) money

5. In the picture, you can see a—

    (A) boy   (B) TV

    (C) cage   (D) car

Kenji had just made a playhouse. The house had three windows and was painted red. Kenji was going to get his friends. He wanted to show them the playhouse. But when Kenji shut the door, the playhouse fell down.

When his father came home, Kenji told him about the playhouse. His father helped him build it again. This time, the house didn't fall down when Kenji shut the door.

1. The best title is—

    (A) Kenji Plays a Game

    (B) Father Goes Away

    (C) A Boy Finds a Home

    (D) Kenji and His Playhouse

2. The story says that Kenji's playhouse had—

    (A) three windows   (B) two TVs

    (C) a green light   (D) four rooms

3. The playhouse fell down when Kenji—

    (A) laughed   (B) shut the door

    (C) ran into it   (D) walked into it

4. Kenji had a good playhouse after—

    (A) his mother   (B) his father
         helped him   helped him

    (C) it rained   (D) he got a cat

5. In the picture, Kenji is—

    (A) working   (B) talking

    (C) painting   (D) walking

Rosa was playing in her house. A truck with boxes of toys was going by. The back door of the truck came open, and all the boxes of toys came out. The man stopped the truck to get the toys.

Rosa ran out of her house. She helped the man put the toys back into the truck. The man said, "Thank you. Take any toy you want for helping me." Rosa took a red ball.

1. The best title is—

   (A) Rosa Helps a Man
   (B) Rosa Rides in a Truck
   (C) Rosa Gets a Pet
   (D) Rosa Plays a Game

2. The truck had boxes of—

   (A) food   (B) toys
   (C) coats   (D) shoes

3. Rosa took a—

   (A) red ball   (B) green coat
   (C) hat   (D) cow

4. When the boxes came out of the truck, Rosa was—

   (A) in her house (B) sleeping
   (C) at school   (D) cutting the grass

5. In the picture, you can see—

   (A) trees   (B) a girl
   (C) a house   (D) a truck

Pam found her sister's old bike. Long ago it had been a pretty, red bike. Now it looked bad. Some parts were missing. No one could ride it.

Pam began to fix the bike. She got some red paint. She got some new tires. She put a new seat on the bike. She worked hard day after day. Soon Pam had a good bike. She could ride it to school.

1. The best title is—

    (A) Pam Rides a Pony

    (B) Pam and Her Cats

    (C) Mother Helps Pam

    (D) Pam Fixes a Bike

2. The old bike looked—

    (A) bad   (B) good

    (C) green   (D) little

3. Pam got some new—

    (A) toys   (B) friends

    (C) books   (D) tires

4. You can tell that Pam wanted—

    (A) some help   (B) a friend

    (C) a bike   (D) a pet

5. In the picture, you can see—

    (A) a paint can   (B) a dog

    (C) two girls   (D) a tree

A farmer had a pig in his truck. He was taking it to his farm. When the farmer stopped for a red light, the pig jumped out of the truck. It ran into a store.

The people in the store were surprised to see a pig. It ran all around the store. At last the farmer caught the pig. He put it into his truck and took it to his farm.

1. The best title is—

   (A) Going on a Picnic

   (B) A Fast Ride

   (C) A Pig Goes into a Store

   (D) Looking at TV

2. The pig ran into a—

   (A) school   (B) house

   (C) fire   (D) store

3. The farmer put the pig into—

   (A) a boat   (B) a bag

   (C) an airplane   (D) his truck

4. The pig was going to live—

   (A) in a school   (B) on a farm

   (C) at a zoo   (D) in a tree

5. In the picture, the man is—

   (A) on a horse   (B) on a bike

   (C) in an airplane   (D) in a truck

Mrs. Cox likes to look at TV. One day, she went to see a TV show being made!

Mrs. Cox was looking at the show being made. A man asked her, "Would you like to be in the TV show?" Mrs. Cox was happy.

The man put Mrs. Cox in the show. He asked her if she liked being on TV. Mrs. Cox said, "Yes, I do. Being on TV is a lot of fun."

1. The best title is—

    (A) Mrs. Cox Gets a New Coat

    (B) Mrs. Cox Goes to Work

    (C) A Fast Race

    (D) Mrs. Cox Goes on TV

2. The story says that Mrs. Cox likes to—

    (A) play games   (B) ride a bike

    (C) look at TV   (D) go on picnics

3. A man asked Mrs. Cox if she would like—

    (A) to be on TV   (B) to eat some food

    (C) a new car   (D) a new dress

4. You can tell that Mrs. Cox—

    (A) has an airplane   (B) likes to read

    (C) wanted to go home (D) had a good time

5. In the picture, the people look—

    (A) cold   (B) wet

    (C) happy   (D) green

In Unit 6, Mrs. Cox got to be on a TV show.

A. Exercising Your Skill

Look at the picture. Tell about it.

- Are the people inside or outside?
- One man is standing up. What are the other people doing?
- Are the people happy or sad?
- Are there any children in the picture?

Talk with your friends. Tell what you see in the picture.

B. Expanding Your Skill

What kinds of shows have you seen? Have you seen a play or show at school? Have you seen an animal show or a puppet show? Think about a show you have seen. If you have not seen a show, think about a show you would like to see. Talk with your friends about shows. Then write five words that name different kinds of shows.

C. Exploring Language

What kinds of TV shows do you see? Think about all the shows you have seen this week. Draw pictures of three TV sets. Write <u>Weekend Morning</u> under the first picture. Write <u>After School</u> under the next picture. Write <u>Night</u> under the last picture. Under each word write a list of TV shows you watched at that time. Are you surprised at how many shows you saw? Now put stars next to the shows you liked best. Then tell your class why you liked these shows the best.

D. Expressing Yourself

Do one of these things.

1. Put on a show with some of your friends. The show can be a play, a circus, a song and dance show, or a puppet show.

2. Act out a part of a TV show that you and some of your friends have seen. Each one of you can take a part. Try to talk like the people in the TV show.

3. Pretend that you are the person on TV who tells about the weather. What is the weather like today? Is it warm, or is it cold? Is the sun shining, or is it cloudy? Is it raining, or is it clear and dry? Think about what the weather is like. Choose the right weather words. Then give your TV weather report.

Mother had a hard time getting Carla up in the morning. Carla liked to stay in bed. Mother said, "I have to think of a way to get Carla out of bed."

The next day, Mother went into Carla's room. She started singing, "Wake up, wake up, sleepyhead." She sang faster and faster.

Carla laughed and jumped out of bed. "Now you have a way to get me out of bed fast," she said.

1. The best title is—

   (A) Carla Goes to School

   (B) Mother Looks at TV

   (C) Mother Gets Carla Up

   (D) Carla Gets a New Bike

2. The story says that Carla liked to—

   (A) cook   (B) play ball

   (C) cut the grass   (D) stay in bed

3. Mother sang—

   (A) and danced   (B) faster and faster

   (C) louder   (D) a sad song

4. You can tell that Mother—

   (A) likes to swim   (B) likes to read

   (C) stays up late   (D) gets up before Carla

5. In the picture, you can see a—

   (A) chair   (B) book

   (C) bed   (D) dog

One day, Louis was sitting down to eat. He saw his horse by the door. Louis said, "Maybe my horse would like to eat with me." He opened the door and called. The horse came into the house. It began to eat with Louis.

Louis liked eating with his horse. Now the horse eats with him every night. Louis says, "It may look funny, but I like eating with my horse."

1. The best title is—

    (A) A Man and His Dog

    (B) A Horse That Ran Away

    (C) A Man Eats with His Horse

    (D) A House for Animals

2. Louis saw his horse by the—

    (A) door   (B) road

    (C) barn   (D) lake

3. The story says that Louis likes to—

    (A) ride a bike   (B) go to school

    (C) make toy boats   (D) eat with his horse

4. You can tell that Louis—

    (A) never rides his   (B) has many pets
        horse

    (C) likes his horse   (D) likes to fish

5. In the picture, you can see a—

    (A) cow   (B) hat

    (C) bus   (D) store

Doris cut the grass for Father. Father gave her some money for working. Doris put the money into an old shoe.

The next day, Doris wanted her money. But she forgot where she had put it. Doris said, "I have lost my money."

Many days after that, Doris went to put on her old shoes. There, in a shoe, was her money. Doris was happy that she had found her money.

1. The best title is—

    (A) Father Goes to Work
    (B) Doris Finds Her Money
    (C) A Girl Helps Her Mother
    (D) Doris Goes Fishing

2. Doris got money for—

    (A) reading a book   (B) looking at TV
    (C) doing homework   (D) cutting the grass

3. Doris put her money into a—

    (A) hat   (B) shoe
    (C) cage   (D) box

4. Doris' money was lost—

    (A) for many days   (B) on a bus
    (C) in the street   (D) at a zoo

5. In the picture, the girl is—

    (A) fishing   (B) reading
    (C) in a house   (D) in a boat

Ben went to the park. He watched the little animals. The next day he went again. This time he had some seeds with him. He fed the birds. The squirrels came over to get some seeds, too.

Now Ben goes to the park every day after work. He always has food for the animals. The birds and squirrels know him now. They come over to him as soon as they see him!

1. The best title is—

   (A) Ben Feeds the Animals

   (B) Ben Gets a Pet Bird

   (C) No Time for Fun

   (D) Ben and the Baby

2. At the park, Ben—

   (A) ate lunch   (B) read a book

   (C) played ball   (D) watched animals

3. Ben goes to the park—

   (A) after school   (B) on his bike

   (C) after work   (D) with his friends

4. You can tell that Ben likes—

   (A) books   (B) little animals

   (C) good food   (D) his work

5. In the picture, there are—

   (A) three girls   (B) three squirrels

   (C) three birds   (D) three men

"My house looks like all the other houses on the street," said Mr. Hill. "I am going to paint my house so it does not look the same." Mr. Hill painted the doors green. Then he painted the rest of the house red.

Many people came to look at Mr. Hill's house. Mr. Hill said, "I like the way my house looks now. It does not look like the other houses."

1. The best title is—

    (A) Mr. Hill Gets a New House

    (B) Mr. Hill Comes Home

    (C) Mr. Hill Paints His House

    (D) Mr. Hill Builds a Barn

2. Mr. Hill painted the doors—

    (A) green   (B) black

    (C) yellow   (D) blue

3. Mr. Hill painted the rest of his house—

    (A) blue   (B) red

    (C) brown   (D) black

4. You can tell that Mr. Hill knows how to—

    (A) fish   (B) fly

    (C) swim   (D) paint

5. In the picture, there are—

    (A) bikes   (B) dogs

    (C) cars   (D) houses

One day, Lisa was playing with a new toy truck. Her cat wanted to play, too. Lisa put her cat into the truck. She made the toy truck go fast. Her cat liked the ride.

That night, her cat got into the truck and went to sleep. Now the cat sleeps in the truck each night. Maybe it wants another ride!

1. The best title is—

   (A) Lisa Helps Her Mother

   (B) A Girl Has a Fast Ride

   (C) Lisa Finds a Lost Pet

   (D) A Cat and a Toy Truck

2. The story says that Lisa has a—

   (A) cat   (B) big dog

   (C) new hat   (D) old bike

3. In the story, Lisa was playing with a toy—

   (A) airplane   (B) truck

   (C) balloon   (D) car

4. You can tell that the cat—

   (A) is green   (B) can talk

   (C) likes the truck   (D) never eats

5. In the picture, you can see a—

   (A) bed   (B) boat

   (C) box   (D) truck

The Second L A P
Language Activity Pages

A. Exercising Your Skill

Look at the picture. Think back to the story in Unit 9. Tell what answer belongs in the box next to each question. The last box is filled in for you.

1. Where is Doris?

2. Why is Doris on the floor?

3. What did Doris do?　Doris found the money.

B. Expanding Your Skill

What do you see in the closet? Read the words in the box. Three of the words tell about things in the picture. One word does not belong. On your paper, write the words that tell about things in the picture. Then try to add two more things to your list. See if your list is like your friends' lists.

boot	Doris	broom	shoe

C. Exploring Language

Pretend you are Doris in the picture. Read the story below about what Doris is thinking. Tell what words can go in the blanks. Then on your paper, write a good title for the story.

Here is one _____ . But _____ is my other shoe? I can't go out with just _____ shoe! Here it is! I'll put it _____ and go outside. Ouch. What is this? Here is my old _____ that I wear when I cut the grass. What a lucky day!

D. Expressing Yourself

Do one of these things.

1. Write or tell a story about something you lost. Your story can tell about these things:

   • what you lost
   • where you looked for it
   • if you found it
   • how you felt

2. Plan a treasure hunt with your friends. Hide something in your classroom. Give hints for the person who is "It" to follow.

3. Draw a picture of each thing you keep in your closet. Write the name of each thing next to its picture.

Tino's mother asked him to go to the store. She told him what to get.

Tino got some apples at the store. He got some dog food too. Then he went back home.

Tino fed the dog. Then Mother said, "Tino, where is the newspaper? I need it now." Tino went back to the store to get it.

UNIT 13

1. The best title is—

    (A) Mother Reads to Tino

    (B) Tino Gets a Pet

    (C) Tino Goes to the Store

    (D) Mother and Tino Have Fun

2. At the store, Tino got—

    (A) a dog   (B) apples

    (C) cake   (D) a toy

3. Mother needed—

    (A) birdseed   (B) the newspaper

    (C) flowers   (D) a book

4. You can tell that Tino has a—

    (A) friend   (B) bike

    (C) dog   (D) cat

5. In the picture, Tino is—

    (A) at the store   (B) at school

    (C) eating an apple (D) at home

Ana went for a walk. She walked up a big hill that had many trees. Soon Ana was lost.

Many people began to look for Ana. They could not find her. Then Rick said, "My dog will find Ana." Rick's dog ran up the hill. Rick ran behind it.

Soon they found Ana. She was sitting under a tree. Ana was happy that Rick and his dog had found her.

1. The best title is—

   (A) Ana Goes to School

   (B) Rick and His Dog Find Ana

   (C) A Girl and Her Pets

   (D) A Dog Runs Away

2. Ana went—

   (A) to a show   (B) to see a friend

   (C) for a walk   (D) for a ride

3. The story says that Ana walked—

   (A) home   (B) to school

   (C) in water   (D) up a hill

4. When Ana was lost, she was—

   (A) not happy   (B) at a zoo

   (C) in a car   (D) a baby

5. In the picture, there are many—

   (A) cats   (B) boys

   (C) trees   (D) girls

It is fun to give friends something on their birthdays. Luis and Bob like to give each other funny things. On Bob's birthday, Luis gave him shoes with peanuts in them. Bob said, "I want to give Luis something funny too."

When Luis' birthday came, Bob gave him a big box. Luis opened it. In the box was a bank that looked like a duck. The duck had a hat on its head. Luis and Bob both laughed.

1. The best title is—

    (A) Father Works on a Farm

    (B) Two Boys Go to a Shoe Store

    (C) Two Boys Have Fun on Their Birthdays

    (D) Mother and Bob Play a Game

2. Luis gave Bob—

    (A) trucks   (B) a TV

    (C) shoes   (D) a horse

3. Bob gave Luis a—

    (A) fish   (B) duck bank

    (C) wagon   (D) coat

4. You can tell that Luis and Bob—

    (A) have sisters   (B) like to cry

    (C) are babies   (D) are friends

5. In the picture, there are—

    (A) balloons   (B) two hats

    (C) two boys   (D) animals

"I like the bears best of all," said Tim. "I love to watch them swim."

"I like them, too," said Lin. "But I want to see some other animals. Let's go look at the lions next. I can see them right over there."

"I'm very hungry," said Father. "Let's go get some food after we look at the lions. There must be a place to eat here at the zoo."

1. The best title is—

    (A) No Bears for Tim

    (B) Tim and Lin Eat Lunch

    (C) Finding Lost Animals

    (D) A Family at the Zoo

2. Best of all, Tim liked the—

    (A) turtles   (B) lions

    (C) bears   (D) fish

3. Tim liked to watch them—

    (A) run   (B) eat

    (C) swim   (D) sleep

4. Father didn't know where the—

    (A) bears were   (B) lions were

    (C) car was   (D) food was

5. In the picture, there are—

    (A) five bears   (B) four people

    (C) two lions   (D) three birds

One day, Mary saw snow all over the ground. She said, "I'm going to make something with the snow."

Mary has a pet cat, so she made a big cat of snow. When she finished, her pet cat jumped on the snow cat's head.

Everyone who saw the two cats laughed. It looked funny to see one cat sitting on another cat.

1. The best title is—

   (A) Looking at TV
   (B) A Good Book
   (C) Fun at School
   (D) Two Funny Cats

2. The cat that Mary made was—

   (A) in a car   (B) little
   (C) lost   (D) made of snow

3. Mary's pet cat sat on the—

   (A) snow cat   (B) school bus
   (C) old boat   (D) little balloon

4. Mary's snow cat was—

   (A) red   (B) white
   (C) green   (D) blue

5. In the picture, the girl is—

   (A) feeding her dog   (B) throwing snowballs
   (C) making a snow cat (D) by a window

Tim and Sara were shooting baskets. Sara made three baskets. Then she missed. Tim made a basket. The ball rolled away.

The dog ran after the ball. He hit the ball with his paw. The ball rolled away. Sara ran after the ball. Tim ran after the ball. The dog got the ball again.

Tim and Sara laughed. "Stop, silly dog," Sara said. "Get the little ball. You play with the little ball. Tim and I will play with the big ball."

1. The best title is—

    (A) The Dog Plays Ball

    (B) Tim and Sara Ride Bikes

    (C) Sara Goes Home

    (D) Tim Has a Dog

2. Sara made—

    (A) a home run   (B) a long jump

    (C) three baskets   (D) a birthday cake

3. In the story, the dog—

    (A) did not eat   (B) stopped playing

    (C) likes to play ball (D) went into the house

4. You can tell that Sara and Tim—

    (A) are in the house   (B) like baseball

    (C) go to school   (D) think the dog is
                                  funny

5. In the picture, the boy is—

    (A) working   (B) playing

    (C) lost   (D) crying

One day, Jean saw the older girls having a race. Jean said, "I am going to be a fast runner, too." She began to run after school. Each day she ran and ran.

The next year, there was a race for all the girls at school. Many of the girls ran fast, but Jean ran faster. She got first prize for being the fastest girl in school.

1. The best title is—

   (A) A Girl Who Can Run Fast

   (B) A Girl Goes Home

   (C) Looking at a Race on TV

   (D) Jean Helps a Goat

2. In the story, Jean saw a—

   (A) duck   (B) big turtle

   (C) race   (D) fast car

3. The story says that each day Jean—

   (A) cried   (B) fished

   (C) jumped   (D) ran

4. When Jean got first prize, she was—

   (A) wet   (B) happy

   (C) cold   (D) lost

5. In the picture, the girl is—

   (A) sitting   (B) running

   (C) walking   (D) swimming

In Unit 19 you read a story about Jean winning a race. Read the story again.

One day, Jean saw the older girls having a race. Jean said, "I am going to be a fast runner, too." She began to run after school. Each day she ran and ran.

The next year, there was a race for all the girls at school. Many of the girls ran fast, but Jean ran faster. She got first prize for being the fastest girl in school.

A. Exercising Your Skill

Look at the story map below. The main idea is missing. Think what the main idea is. Write it on your paper. Draw a circle around it.

1. Jean began to run after school.

2. There was a race at school.

3. Many girls ran the race.

4. Jean ran in the race.

B. Expanding Your Skill

People like to win in sports. Sometimes a whole team wins. Sometimes just one person wins. Make two lists. Write the words below on your paper. Then write or tell the names of other games in each list.

A Team Wins   One Person Wins

baseball   checkers

C. Exploring Language

Read the stories below. Each story has a sentence that tells the main idea. Write the main idea on your paper, or tell it.

1.   The Green Team is the best baseball team. Todd is their best hitter. Jamie is their best pitcher. When Todd and Jamie play, the Green Team always wins. All the other teams hate to play the Green Team.

2.   Ana wants to play ball. She played ball last year. But now she has hurt her foot. The doctor says that Ana can play sometime after her foot gets better. She really wants to play ball again soon.

D. Expressing Yourself

Do one of these things.

1. Have you ever won a prize? Write a story about a prize you have won or a prize you would like to win.

2. Jean ran and ran for a year before she won the race. Make a list of things that take a lot of practice before you are good at them. Put sports and other kinds of things on your list. Give your list a title.

3. Watch a race or game at your school. Draw a picture of the winner. Write a title for your picture.

Mrs. Collins goes for a long walk every morning. She walks down her street. She walks around the park. She goes by the school. Then she walks back home.

Today Mrs. Lopez walked with Mrs. Collins. That made Mrs. Collins happy. "A long walk always helps me feel good," she said. "But a long walk with a friend helps me feel even better."

1. The best title is—

    (A) The Park at Night
    (B) Three Friends
    (C) The Morning Walk
    (D) Mrs. Collins Goes to School

2. Mrs. Collins walks around—

    (A) the school   (B) her friend
    (C) her home   (D) the park

3. A long walk helps Mrs. Collins—

    (A) get sleepy   (B) feel good
    (C) read the paper   (D) get to school

4. On most days, Mrs. Collins walks—

    (A) by herself   (B) with her child
    (C) to school   (D) with her dog

5. In the picture, you can see—

    (A) the school   (B) a hat
    (C) the park   (D) a man

Dom went to bed. Before he went to sleep, he heard something at his window. Dom was afraid.

Dom jumped out of bed. He ran to his mother. "Something is at my window," said Dom. "Please come and look."

Mother went to look. It was Dom's cat. No one had let it in the house that night. Dom laughed. "I was afraid of my own cat."

1. The best title is—

    (A) Mother Goes to Sleep
    (B) A New Toy for Dom
    (C) Why Dom Was Afraid
    (D) Dom Stays Home

2. Dom heard something—

    (A) under his bed   (B) at his window
    (C) in the car   (D) at his door

3. Dom ran to his—

    (A) school   (B) friend
    (C) father   (D) mother

4. You can tell that Dom has a—

    (A) truck   (B) balloon
    (C) pet   (D) boat

5. In the picture, Mother is—

    (A) reading   (B) sitting
    (C) playing   (D) eating

Jill was cutting the grass around her house. She looked and saw a goat. It was eating the grass. Jill told it to go away.

The goat went on eating the grass. Jill could not stop it. She didn't know what to do!

Then a farmer came. He said that the goat was his. It had jumped out of his truck. The farmer took his goat and went away.

1. The best title is—

    (A) Jill and the Goat

    (B) Jill Plays a Game

    (C) A Trip to a Farm

    (D) Goats Like to Play

2. In the story, Jill was—

    (A) painting the house   (B) cooking

    (C) sleeping in bed   (D) cutting grass

3. The goat had jumped out of a—

    (A) car   (B) truck

    (C) wagon   (D) tree

4. When Jill saw the goat, she was—

    (A) surprised   (B) cold

    (C) at dinner   (D) at school

5. In the picture, the goat is—

    (A) sitting down   (B) crying

    (C) under a tree   (D) eating grass

There were four chairs in back of Mr. Smith's house. One day, Mr. Smith painted the chairs red. Then he went into his house.

Before the paint was dry, Mr. Smith's dog jumped all over the chairs.

Mr. Smith came out of the house. He saw what his dog had done. Mr. Smith said, "I should have put my dog in the house. Now I will have to paint the chairs again."

1. The best title is—

    (A) A Cat Helps Mr. Smith

    (B) A Dog Jumps on Mr. Smith's Chairs

    (C) Mr. Smith Gets a New Blue Chair

    (D) Mr. Smith Finds a Boat

2. Mr. Smith painted—

    (A) a bed   (B) his car
    (C) four chairs   (D) two pictures

3. In the story, Mr. Smith went—

    (A) to a party   (B) into his house
    (C) to the store   (D) to a show

4. After the dog jumped on the chairs, the dog's feet were—

    (A) red   (B) blue
    (C) bigger   (D) cut

5. In the picture, the man has—

    (A) a truck   (B) a pet
    (C) books   (D) paint

Joe was going fishing. Mary wanted to go fishing, too. Joe said, "You can't go fishing with me, Mary. You are too little."

Mary said, "I am going fishing, too." She went fishing, but she didn't go with Joe.

That night, Joe and Mary came home. Joe had caught a little fish. Mary had caught three big fish. Joe said, "I guess you are not too little to go fishing!"

1. The best title is—

   (A) Joe Goes Home

   (B) Mary Can Fish

   (C) A Boat Ride

   (D) A Pet Turtle

2. Joe said that Mary was too little to—

   (A) read   (B) paint
   (C) fish   (D) sing

3. Mary caught—

   (A) three big fish   (B) two rabbits
   (C) a dog   (D) two little fish

4. You can tell that Mary—

   (A) caught more fish   (B) is older than Joe
       than Joe
   (C) can not walk   (D) had two boats

5. In the picture, you can see—

   (A) three boys   (B) no fish
   (C) a hat   (D) four fish

There are many cars in Jack's town. Jack was afraid that one of the cars would hit his old dog.

Jack's father said, "I have a friend who lives on a farm. Not many cars go by the farm. Maybe your dog can live there."

Father's friend said that Jack's dog could live on the farm. Jack was happy. Now his dog would not be hit by a car.

1. The best title is—

   (A) Jack's Dog Goes to Live on a Farm

   (B) Father Gets a New Car

   (C) A Boy Who Likes to Work

   (D) Jack Gets a New Pet

2. The story says that in Jack's town there are—

   (A) three schools   (B) no cars

   (C) many cars   (D) many trucks

3. Father's friend lives—

   (A) at a zoo   (B) in a store

   (C) in a truck   (D) on a farm

4. You can tell that Jack—

   (A) can't run   (B) had a party

   (C) likes his dog   (D) likes to play ball

5. In the picture, you can see—

   (A) a girl   (B) a man

   (C) two dogs   (D) a cow

This story was in Unit 23. Read the story again.

There were four chairs in back of Mr. Smith's house. One day, Mr. Smith painted the chairs red. Then he went into his house.

Before the paint was dry, Mr. Smith's dog jumped all over the chairs.

Mr. Smith came out of the house. He saw what his dog had done. Mr. Smith said, "I should have put my dog in the house. Now I will have to paint the chairs again."

A. Exercising Your Skill

Think about how Mr. Smith must have felt at first, when he looked at the chairs he painted. Think about how he felt later, after he saw what the dog had done. Read the lists below. In each list, only two of the words belong. Write the headings on your paper. Then write the two words that belong to each list.

How He Felt at First	How He Felt Later
sad	happy
glad	sorry
happy	sad

B. Expanding Your Skill

Talk about the story with your class. What do you think will happen next?

C. Exploring Language

Read the stories below. On your paper, finish each sentence. First tell what each person makes. Then tell how the person feels.

1.   Lora chopped the nuts. She mixed the flour, eggs, and sugar. Then she poured it all into a pan. Before she put it into the oven, she answered the phone. When she came back, the pan was empty!

    Lora made a _____ . She feels _____ .

2.   Jim used ten colors. He used all his paints. It took all day to finish. Then he hung it up to dry. When he came back, the paint had dripped all over.

    Jim made a _____ . He feels _____ .

D. Expressing Yourself

Do one of these things.

1. Think back to Part A. Draw a picture of the dog. Show how it looked before it jumped on the chairs. Then draw another picture. Show how the dog looked after it jumped on the chairs.

2. Have you ever done something that did not work? Write a story about what happened. Tell how you felt.